S0-AFN-225

María
María

A Story of a Storm

Jennifer Degenhardt

Copyright © 2018 Jennifer Degenhardt
All rights reserved.

ISBN: 0999347969
ISBN-13: 978-0999347966 (Puentes)

DEDICATION

For all Puerto Ricans, either on the island or elsewhere, who have been affected by the storm.

For Sofía Salazar, whose self-awareness, and awareness of the world in general, inspired the character of Kamila. Thank you for being so terrific.

CONTENTS

ACKNOWLEGEMENTS

Thank you to Anabel Pérez Wills, una amiga *boricua*, for not only reading the manuscript and fixing the grammatical errors, but for examining the story with a keen eye for authenticity. A story is only strengthened by the credence with which it is told. Proud of the story as I am, I am even more thrilled for the approval of its authenticity. Thank you, Anabel.

Thank you, too, to Kami Evans. Though we have not (yet!) met, it was she who gave me the idea to write a short novel on Puerto Rico in response to what was happening on the island following the hurricane. With the mere suggestion, it was only hours until I had the story mapped out. I am grateful for the inspiration.

The thanks for the cover art goes to Sklyer Cozine, a 7th grade student (at the time of publication) at the Sanford School in Hockessin, Delaware. And the back cover art was supplied by Alula Díaz an 11th grade student at Fairfield Warde High School in Fairfield, Connecticut. Thank you for your wonderful impressions of a story you hadn't yet read.

To all of the students who participated in the cover art contest for this book, and whose efforts which are seen throughout, thank you for your contributions. Your work is as important to me as I hope mine is to you.

Chapter 1
Kamila

Jack Lazarski, grade 7

It's seven in the morning and we're in the kitchen eating breakfast of *mallorcas*[1], coffee - for my parents and my *abuela*[2] - and milk for me. My *abuela* doesn't live with us, but this morning she is at our house to talk with my *mami*[3].

"Stefany, can you go to Connecticut to help your

---

[1] mallorcas: an eggy and sweet bread topped with powdered sugar.

[2] abuela: grandmother.

[3] mami: mom

sister? She needs you. She is going to have surgery soon. Can you go there for a couple of weeks while she is recuperating?" asks my *abuela*.

"Mamá, I would love to travel to Hartford to help her, but we don't have the money. And I don't have the vacation time at my job to take those two weeks off," my mami explains.

"Can't you talk to your boss at the factory? Doesn't he have family in Hartford, too? Maybe if you explain the situation to him. Susana is your only sister..." says my *abuela*.

"Of course, I know that *mamá*. I want to help Susana. I'll talk to my boss today."

I stay seated at the table. Normally I am a chatterbox, but this morning I don't say a word.

My mami works in one of the companies in our town that produces medical products. The name of our town is San Lorenzo. San Lorenzo is not that big, but it's not that small, either. It's located in the southeast part of the island, less than an hour from the capital of San Juan, depending on the traffic. And a lot of times there is a lot of traffic because the island isn't very big, but still there are a lot of cars and trucks.

Cars and trucks are the only way that products

are delivered to the interior parts of the island. Because the nation is an island there are also many seaports to import necessities. But after the products arrive at the ports, trucks are needed to bring the products to other parts of the island that aren't on the coasts.

Oh, the island where we live? Puerto Rico. The island of enchantment. It is a marvel. It's in the Caribbean, east of the island of Hispaniola, where the Dominican Republic and Haiti are. Puerto Rico is part of the United States. I don't know exactly how or why, but it must be an important topic because my *papi*[4] always talks about the United States government and how it doesn't pay attention to the island of Puerto Rico or its people.

My *papi* knows a lot about politics. He's really smart. He says that many Puerto Rican people - the majority - know a lot about politics; the island in general and how the politicians in Washington D.C. ignore the problems of Puerto Rico. He says that Puerto Rico, though it is a territory of the United States, doesn't have the same representation in the government that the other states have.

My *papi* also works for a corporation located in San Lorenzo. He is a truck driver for a pharmaceutical company. They make really

---

[4] papi: dad.

important medicine in the factories in my town and my *papi* brings them to the seaports and to the airport. From there, the medicine travels on ships to the mainland and to other countries. My *papi* drives on all of the highways of Puerto Rico. He spends a lot of time in his truck so he knows Puerto Rico really well. He always tells us about the poor conditions of the roads in some parts of the island. He complains a lot about the infrastructure. He uses that word a lot. One day we're talking and I ask him about it.

"*Papi*, what is that word infrastr...?" I start to say it, but I can't pronounce it.

"Infrastructure?" he asks.

"Yeah. Infra-struct-ure. I don't understand."

"Kamila," my *papi* explains, "It's a word to describe the systems that exist to support a country."

"What? I don't get it."

"Ok. Listen. Infrastructure consists of buildings, roads and highways and energy sources that are necessary to keep a country operating," he explains.

"So, our house is part of the infra-struct-ure of Puerto Rico?" I ask.

"Yes, in a certain sense. Our family needs a house to live in as much as we need the electricity and the roads for our cars. The Puerto Rican government is happy that we have a house too. If we don't have a house, we are a bigger problem for the political system."

My *papi* continues to talk for ten more minutes that day, but I don't listen too closely because it's boring. I don't like politics as much as my father does.

"Kami, are you ready for school?" my *papi* asks.

*****

My *mami* and her mother continue to talk about my aunt in Connecticut and they don't pay any attention to my *papi* and me.

"Yup, *papi*. Let's go."

We leave the house and get in the truck. Every day my *papi* takes me to school before he goes to work. It's my favorite time of the day: spending time with my *papi*.

Chapter 2
Stefany

I walk to the corner to get the *guagua*[5]. Every day I meet up with the same people from my neighborhood. Some of us work in the medical products industry and others work in the factories that make clothing. I used to work in a clothing factory, but now I'm with a medical company. It's a good job.

This morning I am so distracted because of the problem with my sister and the conversation that I have to have with my boss that I'm not thinking much about the products that the company makes. Still, maybe those products will be ones that they will use in my sister's surgery...

"Stefany, are you coming?" my neighbor, Lucy, asks.
"What? Oh, yeah. Thank you," I answer.

My head is in the clouds. I can't concentrate. I don't want to have this conversation with my boss, but I need to go to Connecticut for two weeks. After her stomach surgery, Susana will have to be in the hospital for five days. After that she can return home, but she won't be able to move for a few days. My sister is young, but the surgery is pretty invasive.

---

[5] guagua: word for "bus" in Puerto Rico.

They have to remove a part of the intestine.

Susana lives in Hartford. It's the capital of the state of Connecticut. She has lived there for the last twenty years. My sister studied finance at the University of Puerto Rico and when she graduated, she got a job as an accountant at one of the insurance firms in Hartford. They say that Hartford is the "Insurance Capital of the World."

We visited her once or twice at her house in the Frog Hollow neighborhood, an area of mostly *boricuas*[6], or Puerto Ricans. And of course, we traveled there to attend her wedding 14 years ago. Susana married Steve, a guy from New York, but they divorced two years ago. She's alone now and that's why she needs help after the operation. Susana and Steve have two kids, too, Justin and Amanda. Though Susana wanted to give them Hispanic names, or at least names that could be pronounced easily in Spanish and English, Steve insisted on giving them English names. It's no surprise that they divorced. No one liked him from the beginning.

*****

The bus arrives at my company. I get off the bus and go in through the main door. I climb the stairs

---

[6] boricuas: nickname for Puerto Ricans.

to go directly to office of my boss, Peter Christensen. He's a man from North Carolina. He speaks Spanish well for having worked here for eight years, but the truth is that I don't like the accent he has when he speaks Spanish.

"Good morning, Mr. Christensen. How are you? I'd like to speak with you. Do you have five minutes?"

With his jarring Spanish accent he responds, "Sure, Stefany. Please come in. How can I help you?" I don't know if it's an issue of respect - or lack of respect - when Mr. Christensen addresses me in an informal manner, or if it's just a lack of control of the language, but it bothers me a little. Anyway, I enter his office. Mr. Christensen offers me a seat and I explain to him what's going on.

Chapter 3
Kamila

Today it's hot, even for Puerto Rico. Normally August is the hottest month of the year and it's humid, too, because of the rain. It rains a lot. With so much rain, there's so much more humidity. It's horrible. But this year, the heat, rain and humidity has continued into September.

In the mornings I get driven to school in my *papi*'s truck, but every afternoon I have to walk the ten blocks to my *abuela*'s house to spend the afternoons with her. In my school uniform - a white shirt, blue skirt and black shoes - I sweat. A lot. I can't wait to get to the house to change my clothes.

I arrive at her small yellow house. When I walk in the door, I am really confused. At the table are my parents and my *abuela*. Everyone seems really serious. It's unusual for my parents to be here because typically it's just my *abuela* who takes care of me until my parents get home from their jobs at five or six o'clock. Yet, it's only four o'clock and everyone is in my *abuela*'s kitchen. Before I open my mouth to ask, my *papi* says to me:

"Kami, sit down. We have to talk to you."

I sit next to my *abuela* and she takes my hand. Besides my *papi*, my *abuela* is my favorite person in the world. She is really caring and funny too. We are good friends because we spend so much time together.

"Kamila." my *mami* says to me. "We have to tell you something. Your Aunt Susana needs an operation immediately. I need to go to Connecticut tomorrow."

"*Tía*[7] Susana? How is she?" I ask them.

"She's in the hospital now. They will operate on her the day after tomorrow. I want to be there to help her. Your cousins are with their father," my *papi* explains.

Until that moment I didn't even think about my cousins. Justin and Amanda are older than me, but I hardly know them. I visited them five years ago in Connecticut and they came to visit us two years ago when they were 11 and 9 years old. But we didn't communicate very well because they don't speak Spanish, and even though I'm learning English in school, I'm still not really good speaking it.

I look at my *mami* and I say to her, "Mami, I don't want you to go. But I'm glad you're helping my *tía*."

"Thank you, Kami. You take care of your papi and *abuela*. Okay?"

"Yes, *mami*. Don't worry."

"Well. Let's go home first to get ready. We'll go

---

[7] Tía: aunt.

out to dinner tonight before my trip."

It's still hot, outside and in the house, but I'm a little chilly because of the news about my *tía* and the change that there will be in our family for a little while.

*****

After the conversation in her kitchen, my parents and I left my *abuela*'s house to return to ours. My *abuela* lives only three blocks from our house on the bank of the Cayaguas River. I like visiting my *abuela*, not only because I love her, but because I like being close to the river.

Her house isn't a typical one for our town. My grandfather built it 50 years ago. It's made of wood and has supports that elevate the house over a part of the river. In one part you can hear the river below. I love that sound. Last year there was a problem with the supports after a rainstorm. But, with the help of a construction company, they fixed it and now the house is okay.

*****

In my room I change into a flowered dress. We're going to a local restaurant in our neighborhood. It's a casual restaurant, but I put on a dress because it's so hot. It's a special night because tomorrow my *mami* is leaving for Hartford.

My *mami*, my *papi* and I first walk to my *abuela*'s house again to pick her up. Afterwards we go to the restaurant, El Coquí. It's really a bar, but it serves food too; food that we like. There are many restaurants and businesses with that same name in Puerto Rico because the *coquí* is a small frog that lives on the island.

We are regulars at the restaurant and the server, Luis, greets us:

"Kamila, Guillermo, Stefany, y *doña*[8] María. How are you tonight?"
"Hi, Luis," I say to him. "We're good, but my *tía* is sick. Tomorrow my *mami* is going to Connecticut."

Luis, a man of fifty-something years, has known us for a long time and he also knows my *tía*.

"What's wrong with Susana?" Luis asks.

My *mami* explains the situation, while Luis brings us to our favorite table close to the window. But first we have to pass through the bar where there is an enormous TV. CNN is on and the journalist with a map behind him explains something about a hurricane. I hear the word "Maria." My *papi* hears it too. He doesn't want to hear anything about any "Maria," but he does want more information about

---

[8] doña: title used with a woman in Spanish.

the storm.

"Luis, what do you know about the storm?" my *papi* asks.

"Guillermo, they say it's a huge hurricane which is on a direct path to the Lesser Antilles. They don't know if it's going to hit Puerto Rico or if it's going to turn to the east."

"I'll turn on the TV again when we get home. Thanks for the information, Luis."

Normally we have a lot of fun at El Coquí, but that night we are too worried and nervous.

Chapter 4
Stefany

After going out to eat, I return home with my husband and Kamila. I need to prepare to leave tomorrow. I am planning on staying in Connecticut for two weeks, but everything depends on my sister's recovery. She needs me and I'm going to be there to help her.

It's a beautiful night. It's no longer hot and there's also a soft breeze. Where we live the sunset is not as spectacular as the sunrise, but tonight it's really pretty. There is a purple and orange light from the setting sun that almost lights up our little house. The whole scene, with the house and the sunlight, fills my heart. Guillermo and I bought the house two years ago, after renting many apartments here in San Lorenzo. I am so proud of the house because of what it took to buy it.

In that light blue house with the brown door is my world. There live the two people who are the most important in my life: my husband and my daughter. The house is not that big, so the rooms aren't either. There are two bedrooms, a living room, a kitchen and a bathroom. It's perfect for us. My favorite time of the day is when we're in the living room in the evening watching TV.

That night when we get home, Guillermo walks in

and goes directly to the living room to turn on the TV. On CNN, the same journalist is explaining something about what's happening in the Middle East, so my *papi* changes the channel to The Weather Channel. The meteorologist has a map behind her showing the hurricane's route - the hurricane that formed a week ago in the Atlantic Ocean and which is now headed towards the smaller islands of the Caribbean. The last time that we had a hurricane was in 1998 when Hugo landed on the island. They say that that hurricane was a Category 1 storm, but because of the amount of rain - 30 inches in two days - the island's infrastructure suffered a lot. Though I was only 9 years old - the same age as Kamila is now - I remember well the destruction in Puerto Rico and how we suffered for a long time afterwards.

Guillermo says to me:

"Oh my God. Look at the path of this storm. It seems like it's coming directly for the island. There's no escaping it."

My husband loves to watch TV. A lot of the time he likes to watch sports, soccer in particular, but when there is a potential disaster, he loves to be glued to the TV to see what's happening, minute by minute. That is one of the disadvantages of the news today: because of satellites, the internet and cell phones, people know information exactly when something happens. Sometimes it's good to have the information, like when there's an issue with the highways, but other times it's not as helpful. Of course, people want to know about a hurricane that's headed for their nation so they can prepare, but I imagine that having all of the facts ahead of the storm can also cause panic. Yet maybe it's only me who's panicking because I'm not going to be with my family when the storm arrives.

I say to my husband with as much love as I can, "Guillermo, can you please lower the volume on the TV? You know I don't like to hear so much bad news. Besides, I'm leaving tomorrow and I am worried."

Guillermo is a tall, big Puerto Rican, but he is also very sweet. He takes my hand and gives me a huge hug.

"Stefany, don't worry. Everything is going to be okay. I am going to take care of Kami and your *mamá* while you're in Connecticut. You know how much I love you and how much I'm going to miss you."

I have so much to do to pack and to get ready for the trip, but I just want to stay there in my husband's embrace.

"Thank you, Guillermo. I love you, too. I trust you, always. Now, let me go get ready for tomorrow."

I give my husband a kiss and I thank him silently. This man is my world and I love him with all of my heart, as much as I love my daughter who happens to be in her room listening to music.

"Kami, what are you doing?" I ask her.
"Listening to music," she answers me.
"Is it a new song? I've never heard it," I say to my daughter.
"It's new to me, Mami. The song is called "*Hijos del Cañaveral*." Amelia told me about it yesterday. I like it. Do you?"

Kamila wants to talk more, but the truth is that I don't have time. But still, I don't want to move from the doorway of her room.

"Kami, we'll listen to the song after my trip. Now I have to get ready to go tomorrow."
"Ok, Mami."

I take one more look at my daughter before going into my bedroom. Once there I take out the suitcase and I begin to fill it up.

Chapter 5
Kamila

Fendi Hartke, grade 6

"Kamila, wake up," my *papi* says from the doorway of my room. "You have to get ready for school. We're going to drop you off first and then your *mami* and I will go to the airport."

I don't want to get out of bed because I'm still sleepy, but I wake up enough to ask my father, "Can't I go to the airport with you?"

"No. You have to go to school like always. And in the afternoon you'll help your *abuela* get ready."

Now I'm sitting on the bed with my feet touching the floor. "Get ready? For what? Mami is leaving today."

"The hurricane that has already landed on the other small islands in the Caribbean is headed directly for Puerto Rico. The storm is going to be really severe, so we have to be ready. You and your *abuela* are going to start this afternoon and I will come and help when I get back from work later on.

"Ok, *papi*. I'll help *abuela*. What do we have to do?

"*Abuela* will show you this afternoon. Now, shower, brush your teeth and get dressed."

Normally my *papi* is really funny; only sometimes is he serious. This morning he seems really serious. He must be worried because my *mami* is traveling. Or maybe he's worried about the hurricane. I don't know. We've had hurricanes before. It's normal to live a few days without lights and electricity after a big storm. My *papi* says it's because of the infrastructure. I still don't understand that word.

I don't think about it anymore. I take my backpack and walk into the kitchen to have breakfast with my parents. My *abuela* is not there that morning. She's probably at her house with her birds. Since my *abuelo*[9] died seven years ago, my *abuela* has lived with her feathered friends.

After a silent breakfast, the three of us get in the

---

[9] abuelo: grandfather.

truck to go to my school. I sit between my parents and I try to explain to them that it is a special occasion that my *mami* is traveling and I want to say good-bye to her at the airport, but they don't listen to my complaints.

I give my *papi* a kiss and my *mami* and I get out of the truck. She says to me, "Kamila, you know I love you with all of my heart. I'm going to miss you a lot. Take care of yourself and be good for your *papi* and *abuela*. See you in a couple of weeks."
"Mami, I'm going to miss you too. Everything is going to be okay. Don't worry."

And with those words I give my *mami* a big hug and I walk to the front door of the school.

*****

The whole day all of the adults talk about Hurricane Maria. Maria. Every time I hear that name I think of my *abuela*. Her name is María Josefina, but everyone just calls her María.

With the instructions from my parents, I get to my *abuela*'s house after school. She is outside with the hose filling bottles with water.

"Hi, *abuela*," I greet her.
"Kami, love. Come help me."

My *abuela* is nice, but sometimes she's a little

demanding. But when I am close to her, she gives me a hug and a kiss.

"Okay, okay, *abuela*. What are you doing?"

"We have to prepare a lot, Kamila. The hurricane that's coming is huge."

"They say that every time there's a storm."

"No, this time it's different. The meteorologists say that it's already a category 4 storm and it's getting stronger every day. We need to prepare."

"Ok, *abuela*. I'll help you. And after, can I go out and play with Amelia?"

"We'll see. Now, help me fill these bottles and bring them inside."

That afternoon I can't go out to play with Amelia. My *abuela* and I work filling the bottles with water, looking for candles and matches and doing other things to prepare for the storm.

Chapter 6
Stefany

When we were younger, Guillermo used to borrow his brother's truck and we would drive around for hours. Most of the time we would go to Fajardo or to San Juan because those cities are close to San Lorenzo. And one time we went to Mayagüez for the weekend. We took the southern route and stopped in Ponce for lunch. After a few hours in the truck, we arrived in Mayagüez and spent two beautiful days at the beach.

But it didn't matter where we were going then or where we are going now, we always talk a lot when we're riding in the car. But this morning it's different. I don't talk to my husband because I don't want to start crying. Finally, Guillermo speaks:

"Stefany. I want you to know that everything is going to be okay, with your sister and with us here. I will take care of our family. You only need to worry about your sister," he says. "Justin and Amanda are going to be with Steve, right?"

"Yes. They are going to stay with him for a few weeks. But I'm going to bring them to the hospital because Susana will want to see them after the operation."

"Of course. And when is the operation?" Guillermo asks.

"Tomorrow morning," I reply.

I really don't want to have any conversation, but it is easier to think about what I have to do to take care of my sister instead of worrying about my family. I'm leaving them for a long time, just when his hurricane is about to arrive.

I would prefer to arrive at the airport quickly, but it's impossible with the traffic today. Luis Muñoz Marín Airport is only 40 kilometers from San Lorenzo, and normally it takes less than an hour to get there. Today, the trip is longer, but I will still arrive with enough time to make my flight, which isn't until one o'clock in the afternoon. We're going early because it's easier for Guillermo to bring me now because he has to go to San Juan to pick up a shipment there to bring it back to the company in San Lorenzo.

Without saying anything, I look out the window of the truck and I see the beauty of my island. That morning there are white clouds in the sky, the very sky that seems connected to the little mountains and hills that we pass by on our way to the airport. The morning is cool, but you can tell already that it's going to be hot in the afternoon. I look at the small houses and the apartment buildings with the clothes drying on the clotheslines outside. I like to look at the clothes on the line because it shows that people live there. Signs of life. At that hour the palm trees sway in the breeze. I think to myself; I could never move away from Puerto Rico like my sister. I love living here.

The good-bye at the airport is hard. I can't control my tears because I don't want to leave my husband. As usual, he kisses me on the forehead:

"Stefany, I love you. Take care of yourself."

I walk into the airport to take a direct flight to Bradley International Airport in Hartford.

Chapter 7
Kamila

Ava Swann, grade 5

Again, my *papi* has the TV tuned to CNN. The newscasters continue talking about the storm that is coming to the island of Puerto Rico. The weather person giving the report that morning says that the hurricane landed on the island of Dominica to the southeast. He shows images of just before the storm arrived on the tiny island of 70,000 people. The wind there must be really strong because the palm trees are almost bent in half.

"The hurricane named Maria has a small eye, indicating that the storm is stronger than normal.

You can see in the video here that only 24 hours ago there were winds of 90 miles per hour, but were increasing in intensity. The meteorologists from the National Weather Service say that this storm could become a category 5."

The newscaster continues:

"We don't have video from the island of Dominica, but we've received information that there is total destruction on the island. Now, Maria is on a course headed directly for Puerto Rico. It will be necessary to heed warnings and prepare yourselves in order to protect life and property."

I go into the living room where my *papi* is watching TV. He seems worried.

"Papi, do you have to work today?" I ask him.
"No, Kami. They say that the hurricane is going to arrive in a day or so and there is much to do to prepare. I need to secure our house and your *abuela*'s. This is going to be a horrible storm for Puerto Rico."

The journalist interrupts our conversation with new information:

"According to the information that we are receiving from the National Weather Service, the hurricane is fluctuating between a category 4 and

category 5."

Another man comes on the TV screen, an official from Puerto Rico. He mentions that there are still 60,000 to 80,000 customers who still don't have electricity after Hurricane Irma which hit the island only days ago.

Normally I wouldn't worry because the weather in Puerto Rico doesn't change much. It's always hot and humid which is, at least for us *boricuas*, comfortable. And sometimes there is rain and an occasional storm. But my *papi* seems worried, so I start to get nervous.

"What are we going to do, *papi*?"
"Everything is going to be okay. Let's go first to your *abuela*'s house to help her."

* * * * *

We walk the few blocks to get to my *abuela*'s house. On the way we see many of the neighbors getting ready. *Señor*[10] Alonzo is covering his car with a sheet of plastic, and *Señora*[11] Lucas is bringing her plants inside from the patio. It's hard work for her because she has so many plants. On a regular day, *Señora* Lucas spends a lot of time tending to her beautiful plants. It seems like a good idea to bring

---

[10] señor: mister.
[11] señora: missus.

them inside. We greet her when we pass by her house.

"Hi, *Señora* Lucas. Good luck with your plants. Do you need any help?" my *papi* asks.

My *papi* has a good heart. He is always helping other people.

"Thank you, Guillermo. I only need help with this big one. Can you help me?"

We step onto *Señora* Lucas's patio. While my *papi* lifts the heavy plant, *Señora* Lucas and I take some small plants and follow my *papi* to the living room of the house.

"There you are *Señora* Lucas. Do you have everything you need for the duration of the storm?"

"Yes. Thank you. Yesterday my son came from Bayamón to check on the rest of the house, the windows and the roof. He wanted me to return with him, but I wanted to stay here," *Señora* Lucas replies.

"Good. Hopefully the storm will pass quickly. They say it is a huge storm."

"Yes. That's what I saw on CNN and on The Weather Channel. I hope the island is ready."

"Well, *Señora* Lucas, we have to go and help my mother-in-law. We have to secure her house and bring her to ours for the duration of the storm. Call us if you need us."

"Good. Thank you, Guillermo. And thank you, Kamila, for your help with the plants."

"You're welcome, *Señora* Lucas. Bye," I say to her.

My *papi* and I continue on to my *abuela*'s house.

Abuela is outside cleaning one of the cages for the many parrots she has. The birds only like my *abuela* so when they see us or smell us, they start to make noise.

"Hi, María," my *papi* says to my *abuela*. "Why are you not getting the house ready?"

"Hi, Guillermo. Hi, Kamila."

My *abuela* stops a second to give me a big hug and kiss on the cheek. She has the same name as the Virgen Maria and is as strong as her, too. But I imagine that my *abuela* is more regimented, and is definitely more stubborn. She responds objectively to my *papi*'s question:

"Guillermo, you know that I clean the cages on Tuesdays and today is Tuesday. Ramón y Rocío and the other birds need a clean house too."

It seems like my *papi* wants to get mad at my *abuela*, but there's no time. There is too much to do.

"Okay, María. I'm going in the house to check it out. Finish what you're doing and then we'll go to our house to wait out the storm," my *papi* says.

"Guillermo, I can't leave the birds alone in the house. I'm staying here. The storm will pass quickly. You can come to check on me later. If I need you, I'll call you."

"Oh, María. You can't stay here alone. They say that the winds will be up to 150 miles per hour - or more. It's not safe to stay here alone. You need to come with us. I promised Stefany that I would take care of the both of you."

"Guillermo, you know that I love you like my own son and you've always been good to me. But the truth is, I'm not leaving this house. I have endured many storms in this house, with my husband and alone, and this time I'm staying here. I'm not changing my mind. Thank you for your concern, but everything is going to be okay."

My *papi* tries to convince my *abuela* for another ten more minutes, but she's not budging. She has it in her mind that she wants to spend the night with her birds and that is what she is going to do. Finally, I give her a big hug. My *papi* gives her a hug, too, and when he lets go, he also gives her a kiss on the forehead and says, "Take care of yourself, María. I'll call you to check in."

Though I'm really too old to do it, when my *papi* takes my hand to hold it while we walk home, I let him. I don't know what's going to happen the following day when the hurricane arrives, but I want to be near my *papi.*

Chapter 8
Stefany

On the plane I find myself sitting between an older woman and a businesswoman. The businesswoman in her black suit, and carefully arranged hair and red lipstick doesn't even greet me as I sit down. She merely opens her computer to starts to do some work, preparing for a meeting, I imagine. Though I don't feel like talking to anyone (and for that reason I'm not bothered that the woman doesn't speak with me), the *abuelita*[12] in the other seat begins to tell me the story about why she's traveling to Hartford, who she's going to visit and how long she's going to be there. The flight from the airport in San Juan to Hartford is three hours and the old lady talks to me for the entire time.

The last time I traveled to Connecticut, the airline served us food, but this time the flight attendants only offer us a little snack and a drink. It doesn't matter, though, because I'm not hungry. I don't have a lot of experience flying so I'm nervous. But I'm also worried about my family: my family in Puerto Rico and my sister who is already in the hospital in Hartford. My family is preparing for the hurricane that's coming while my sister prepares for her own hurricane.

---

[12] abuelito: literally, "little grandmother"; here: old lady.

Interrupting my thoughts and my worries, the old woman, whose name is Julia, says to me:

"What part of Puerto Rico are you from?"

It must be nerves, but this woman can talk. She only gives me the opportunity to say, San Lorenzo, when she starts to tell me that her parents gave her the name of Julia because of the young girl, Julia Vázquez Torres. That young woman, long ago, at twelve years old, had supernatural powers that she used to help people. The legend continued: Julia used plants and with the pure water of a well, she cured many illnesses of the people of the region. Julia's parents were so impressed by the story, and since they were living close to San Lorenzo in the city of Caguas at the time, they decided to name their daughter after the young woman who had the powers of healing.

Once, when the older woman stopped long enough to breathe, I asked her, "And did you work in medicine like the young girl?"
"Oh, no. Before retiring, I worked at the mall selling clothes."

I don't say anything about the missed opportunity of not studying medicine like her namesake, but I don't want to chat any longer. Again, I start to think about Kamila, Guillermo and my *mamá*, but I don't have a moment to rest when the woman starts talking again.

"What do you think about this Hurricane Maria? They say it's going to be really serious and we're lucky that we left the island today."

"Yes," I answer her. "It's fortunate that we left today. But the truth is that I am worried about my family still in Puerto Rico."

"What a shame, *hija*[13]," Julia says to me. "Why are you traveling to Connecticut?"

It's only the second real question that Julia has asked me in almost two hours of traveling. Though it makes me smile when she pronounces the name of the state where we're going as Conn-EC-ti-cut, with a lot of emphasis on the vowels, I don't tell her that is not the way to pronounce it. I'm so tired. I am so tired that I don't even want to answer her, but she has been so nice to me that I want to be compassionate, so I explain to her everything that is going on in my life. At least it's an opportunity to express myself. And that's the way we pass the last hour of the flight.

I don't pay a lot of attention to the conversations that are happening on the plane, but I can tell that many people are talking about the storm. There's a

---

[13] hija: literally, "daughter"; here used a term of endearment

guy, obviously a *gringo[14]*, who is talking so loudly about the luck of being able to leave the island before the hurricane arrived. He's a guy between 40 and 50 years old who has obviously spent a lot of time outside because his skin is the color of a red tomato. He's also wearing a New England Patriot's hat and a yellow shirt with purple palm trees and green beer bottles. A true tourist. It seems like he has needed the flight attendant's assistance every five minutes. It's hard to concentrate on any other conversation because he talks so much and is so loud. But no one wants to tell him to shut up. We learn that he's from Springfield, Massachusetts, that he loves football and that he travels a lot to the Caribbean. He's a walking stereotype of a tourist from the mainland.

In San Lorenzo there aren't as many tourists as there are on the coasts of the island, but there are some. The people who come to San Lorenzo normally come to visit people who work in the pharmaceutical companies, and from there they visit the beaches. Listening to that tourist I'm even more grateful that we don't live close to any of the famous beaches so I don't have to encounter any guys like this red-faced tourist.

Finally, the plane lands at Bradley International.

---

[14] gringo: word referring to an American who is not Hispanic or Latino

The man from Massachusetts is in a hurry and he pushes his way through so he can get off the plane first.

When I finally get off the plane, I'm attacked by a headache at the very moment I arrive at the taxi area.

"To Hartford Hospital, please."

My sister is waiting for me there.

Chapter 9
Kamila

My papi and I walk the few blocks between our house and my grandmother's, a walk that is difficult that night because of the wind and the rain. They say that when the eye of the hurricane passes through a place is when it finally arrives. But they also say that a hurricane, and this one in particular, is larger than its eye and because of that, the winds are so strong before the actual arrival of the storm.

It's really windy. There's no one on the streets that we can see, and for good reason. The palm trees are bending a lot with the wind and everything that is not tied down is blowing through the air.

With one more block until we get home, my papi receives an alert on his phone. Out of habit, he checks his phone, though with more difficulty because he's also holding my hand. He reads the message:

There are shelters available in the public schools in every city for the residents that need them. Please take care of yourself in this storm. There will probably not be power for some days after the hurricane passes due to the winds of more than 150 MPH.

My *papi*'s face looks even more worried. "What does it say, *papi*?"

"It's nothing, Kami. They say the storm is really big and the situation on the island is really serious."

I don't say anything else to my papi until we get home. Though there are a lot of storms that hit the island a lot, normally the newscasters don't spend so much time talking about them. I don't typically like to watch the news, but for several days I have seen it everywhere in my life, from the TVs at home, at school and in the restaurants, and even the announcement that I see on my iPod Touch. It's evident that this hurricane is so different from others, and because of that, I'm afraid.

We walk in the house and we get ready for a long night. My *papi* tries to act like it's a normal night even though it isn't.

"Kami, do you want to play *lotería*[15]? he asks me.
"*Papi, lotería* isn't a game for two people. You know that," I answer.
"You're right. Normally we play with your *mami* and grandmother. Ok. A different game?"
"Yeah. Let's play cards. We'll play *pares*[16]."

Pares is a game where the players need to make pairs with the cards that are the same, for example, two "nines" or two "kings."   The player with the

---

[15] lotería: Spanish version of the game "bingo."
[16] pares: card game similar to "Go Fish."

most pairs at the end wins the game. My *papi* and I both know it's a game for little kids, and that I'm really too old to play, but neither of us says anything. Other than being an easy game to play to calm me down, I am enjoying the memories of when I used to play when I was young. And my *papi* is happy to play, too.

The TV is on, and while we're playing cards we watch programs with news of the hurricane. Though my *papi* doesn't have the sound turned on, we see the images of destruction that the storm has caused in other places, and maps of the route it's taking. They say that Maria is going to arrive by six the next morning.

We can hear the wind outside. It sounds like a fast train passing by. When it blows hard, we almost can't hear anything else. And with the rain hitting the roof... I have no idea what to think. I get up from the couch and I go to the window to look outside. In that very moment the power goes out. The TV shuts off. The house lights turn off and the streetlights, too. The darkness is complete. Nothing else can be heard except the wind and the rain.

"I'm afraid, *papi*. I don't want anything to happen to us."

My *papi* doesn't hear me because he's in the kitchen getting candles and matches. He comes back to the living room with two lit candles.

"Kami, come sit with me. I know that you're afraid, but everything is going to be okay. We have survived many storms and we'll survive this one, too. I'm going to call your grandmother if there's still service."

Taking the phone, my *papi* tries to call my *abuela* at her house. I think about my *abuela* and how much I love her, but I also think about how stubborn she is. She should be with us right now.

"I can't get through," my *papi* says as he pushes the button to end the call. "There's no service. May God bless Maria, and us. All of us."

Those last two sentences my *papi* whispers, but I heard everything he said. Hearing those words, I realize the severity of the situation because my *papi*, one of my favorite people in the world, isn't religious.

We sit on the couch listening to the noise going on outside until I fall asleep.

Chapter 10
Stefany

At the hospital I go to my sister's room and greet her with a kiss and a hug. She's in the bed waiting for surgery. She is really tired and seems like she's in pain so she doesn't say much to me, but she asks me immediately about our *mamá* and what's going on with the hurricane.

"Stefany, how's *mamá*?"

"She's okay, Susana. I left her with Guillermo and Kamila. Everything is going to be okay. I talked with Guillermo when I got off the plane. He was going with Kami to *mamá*'s house to bring her to our house to wait out the storm."

"Good. How are you? Thank you for coming," Susana says to me.

"It's nothing, Susana. It's a pleasure to be able to help you. I'm fine," I answer her.

The truth is that I'm not fine. I'm worried; definitely not okay. I am worried about my family; my daughter whose only nine, my husband and my mother. And I'm also worried about my sister who's in the hospital, getting ready for an invasive surgery the next morning. But, because I'm only one person, I focus on the most immediate worry: my sister.

"Can I get you something, Susana? I'm going to

get some food in the cafeteria. What do you need?"

"No. Thank you, Stefany. I don't need anything. I'm going to close my eyes for a bit. The stomach pain is draining my energy."

"Okay, Susana. Rest. I'll be right back," I say to her.

I leave her room in search of the cafeteria. I ask a hospital employee where the elevator is to get to the cafeteria.

"At the end of the hall on the right," he says.

Of course. I wasn't paying attention when I arrived, but now I realize that I did see a sign with directions to the cafeteria.

In the cafeteria I buy an egg salad sandwich, a salad and a soda. I'm not hungry, but I know it's necessary to eat to keep up my strength. In the cafeteria there is a TV tuned to CNN. The newscaster is different from the one saw in the airport in San Juan, but she talks even more seriously about what's happening in Puerto Rico and gives predictions about what's going to happen. I feel a knot in my stomach thinking about what's happening on my island. Yes, I'm safe here, but my world, my family, is there.

I finish eating the sandwich and because I can't eat anymore, I save the salad for later. I go up to check on my sister before going to her house for the night.

Chapter 11
Kami

Zi Burns, grade 8

CRACK!

CRASH!

The sound wakes me in an instant.

"*Papi!*" I call to my *papi*, afraid. "What happened?"

My *papi* is awake and is standing at the window watching the storm.

"Kami, it's okay. Don't worry."
"But, what was it?" I ask my *papi*.
"Must have been a big branch that fell from a tree."
"There are no trees close to the house," I mention to my *papi*. "How?" I ask him.
"The wind is really strong, Kami, because the eye of the storm is almost here. And the bands around the eye of a hurricane are the strongest."

Again, we hear a sound. It seems like God is playing the drums on the houses and on other buildings close to our house, without any regular rhythm.

I get up from where I was sleeping. I see the clock on the wall. It says it's 4:30 in the morning. I realize then that I only slept five hours. Last night my *papi* told me that the storm Maria was going to arrive a little after six AM. Still an hour and a half to go.

I can't really see anything from the windows of the house because the lights are out in the street, but I can hear a rain that I've never heard in my life. It's a constant sound. The rain falling from the sky hits the aluminum roof hard. It's scary.

"*Papi*. And, my *abuela*?"

"We will check on her, but later. We can't leave the house now. It's too dangerous."

I think about my *abuela* and I worry about her. It's true that she's strong, but she's old, too. She's alone in her house with her birds. She must be afraid.

"*Papi*, I'm really worried about *abuela*. I hope she's okay."

"I know, Kami. But your *abuela*, though she's stubborn, she's also a tough woman. Think instead about what you're going to do with her after the hurricane."

"Good idea," I respond.

My *abuela* and I spend every afternoon together after school. I like to spend time with her because she doesn't treat me like a baby. She's also a good storyteller. All my life my *abuela* has been telling me stories about her life when she was young and when she lived with my *abuelo*. She tells about my *abuelo*'s strong opinions about politics and the situation in Puerto Rico. Though I don't understand it all, it's obvious from her descriptions that my *abuelo*, when he was alive, still thought that Puerto Rico was a colony of the United States, even though it's been part of the country for a long time. My *abuela* has the same opinions as her husband even so many years after his death. One day she told me:

"Kami, Puerto Rico is an island of contradictions.

At the same time that it's Caribbean, it's also American. It's cosmopolitan and it also suffers from poverty. We are part of the United States but for a hundred years *bregamos*[17] with our identity."

"*Abuela*, what does *bregar*[18] mean?" I ask her.

"*Bregar* means working and persevering against an internal or external struggle. The Puerto Rican people are happy and diligent, but this dichotomy of being Puerto Rican and American has existed for years."

"Dichotomy? What's that?"
"Kami, come here. I'll explain it to you."

That day my *abuela* told me more about the history of the island, a history that she's been a part of for many years.

---

[17] bregamos: we persevere.
[18] bregar: to persevere.

Chapter 12
Stefany

I didn't sleep well thinking about my sister in the hospital and my family in San Lorenzo. I turn on the TV at my sister's house and learn more about the hurricane.

The newscaster from the CNN offices in Atlanta, talks about images that show everything that I need to know at that point: my beautiful island won't ever be the same as it once was. There are video clips of rivers swollen with the rain pulsing through the streets, and in those waters are roofs of houses and tree branches that have been stripped of their leaves. At that moment I send a text to Guillermo:

-Honey, are you all okay?

My telephone makes the sound to indicate that the text has been sent and I wait for a response.

Before leaving the house I listen to a bit more of the CNN program talking about the storm. The journalist says that the winds have reached 155 miles per hour and that there is no electricity on any part of the island. It doesn't surprise me that my husband doesn't respond, but it worries me just the same.

Though it's really hot in Hartford, I take my

sweater because the hospital is cold because the of air conditioning, and since I'm going to be there all day...

I walk down the steps of the house and greet the Uber driver who is there waiting to take me to the hospital.

Chapter 13
Kamila

It's morning. The storm finally arrived and the situation is really bad. My *papi* and I are in the bathroom waiting until it passes because the wind is horrible. We spend the time listening to the hurricane beating on the island. *Papi* doesn't say much and that's unusual. I know the situation is serious because of the look on his face.

"*Papi*, I'm afraid."

"Don't worry, Kamila. We're okay. Let's sing a little bit, okay?"

"Sure, *papi*. What should we sing?"

"What song do you like?" my *papi* asks.

With the clamor of the hurricane, it's almost impossible to hear ourselves, but the two of us sing "*Lamento Borincano*" and "*Raza de Mil Colores*" many times. They are songs that we play every Sunday at our family meal. They express the pride we have for Puerto Rico. Normally I don't think a lot about the lyrics of the songs, but just then I remember the conversations that my parents and my *abuela* would have after lunch almost every Sunday. My *abuela* would talk the most, as usual:

"Stefany, your father was 'the son of Borinquen'

as the song mentions. He was a *jíbaro*[19] just like his parents and ancestors who came from the countryside. Like them, your father - my beloved husband - worked as hard as all *campesinos*[20] do, but with happiness. He was a man who was proud of the land he came from.

That day my *mami* agreed completely with what her *mamá* said. I saw my *mami* looking at the photo that we have of her and her father in the kitchen. She commented:

"I miss my *papi*. He was such a great man. And I loved to watch how you and he got along, *Mamá*. You were so in love."

My *abuela* said, "Stefany, I miss him too. He was the love of my life," my *abuela* says. "But the relationship that you and Guillermo have reminds me of the love that my Jacobo and I had."

That day the adults talked a lot about Puerto Rico and politics, so I asked for permission to go out and play in the street because I don't like to talk about those things.

*****

---

[19] jibaro: Puerto Rican word to refer to people who work the land in the countryside

[20] campesinos: word to describe people from the countryside.

CRACK!

Something hits the window and breaks the glass.
"PAPI!" I scream.
"Easy, Kami. Take it easy. It's nothing."

With those words my *papi* hugs me even harder and we wait.

*****

Throughout the day we're scared. Not much changes for many hours. I stand up to stretch and I look through the window of the bathroom. Our house is on a hill and I can see the whole street.

Everything is destroyed. There is a huge flood in the street. In some places you can only see the roofs of cars, and some of the houses no longer have roofs: the Martínez's and Mr. Cobán's house. The Martínezes have two little babies. Twins. Where are they? And Mr. Cobán is an old man. Really old. Is he still there at his house?

With a shaky voice I say to my *papi*, "Mr. Cobán's house doesn't have a roof. We need to help him."
"Come, sit down, Kamila. Don't worry. Mr. Cobán is with his family in Ponce. His son arrived three days ago to pick him up."
"*Papi. Abuela*?" I ask him. Thinking of Mr. Cobán makes me think about my *abuela*. I hope she's okay. I'm so worried.

I start to cry. My *abuela*. How is she? Is she okay?

"*Papi*, I want to go see my *abuela*. When can we go?"

"Kami, we can't go now. Later, though, I will go check on her."

The hours of waiting seem like an eternity.

Chapter 14
Stefany

Susana is awake and ready for surgery when I arrive at the hospital. She looks tired and in pain, but she greets me with a smile.

"Stefany, good morning. How did you sleep?"
"Hi, Susana," I say, giving her a kiss on the cheek. "How are you? Good to see you. Are you ready?

Neither one of us responds to the questions of the other. We're nervous - she for the surgery and I for my family and for our mother. I'm even nervous for the island.

Susana has the TV turned to the news channel. She starts talking to me about the hurricane and how Puerto Rico is suffering.

"Did you hear from Guillermo?" she asks.
"No. I sent him texts and tried to call, but I couldn't connect. I'm dying to know how he is."

I don't want to bother my sister with my worries because she is going to be operated on in an hour. She needs to be of sound mind, so I change the subject. We talk a little about her kids, their activities and school - easy things - until a group of nurses arrives to take her to the operating room. From that moment I'm left alone with my thoughts, and the mental exhaustion overtakes my body. I start to cry.

I spend the day motionless in the chair waiting for news, news from my family and from the doctors. The hours seem like an eternity.

Chapter 15
Kamila

We spend a long time in the bathroom, my *papi* and I. I listen to a little bit of music on my iPod until it loses its charge. I play the song *"Hijos del Cañaveral"* on repeat. The singer, Residente, a Puerto Rican rapper, sings about the history of the island and the strength of the people. I'm not that old yet, but after this storm, I know that the island is going to need a lot of that strength.

"Kami, I'm going to try to go to your *abuela*'s house. I want to see if she's okay. I don't want you to come with me. Will you be okay here by yourself?" my *papi* asks me.

"Yes, *papi*. I'll be okay. Thank you for going. Give her a hug. And be careful."

For many hours the rain pounds not only the roof of the house, but the entire island of Puerto Rico. I watch my *papi* put on a rain jacket that probably won't be of much help.

Without music and without enough light to read, I'm left in the bathroom to think. I think about my *mami* with my *tía* so far away. She must be worried about all of us. Parents who are *abuelos* are very special to all Puerto Ricans, but my *abuela* is even more special to my *mami*. My *mami* has so much respect for her mother, and I do, too.

My *abuela* is a storyteller who sometimes stretches the truth, but she's very intelligent. She worked all of her life in a factory, but she always read a lot of books and still does. What she likes best is Pre-Columbian history, especially of Puerto Rico. Last week she taught me more about the Taínos.

"Kamila, you have to learn about the ancestors of our island. The Taínos were indigenous people who had been living here for many years before the arrival of Christopher Columbus."

"Yes, *abuela*. You've told me before. What happened to them again?" I asked my her.

"Many of them died because of the illnesses that the Spanish brought to the island then. But before then, they were a great, organized society that demonstrated skills in engineering."

"Like what?" I asked her.

"Kami, look at that hammock there."

"I love that hammock, *abuela*. We spend a lot of time resting in the hammocks here on your patio."

"Yes, that's true. But, did you know that the hammock is from the Taínos? The Spanish discovered this way of sleeping when they arrived here. The Taínos suspended the hammocks between the trees in order to escape the insects and small animals that crawled on the ground."

"Oh. I had no idea. That's interesting."

"Another Taíno word is *huracán*, (hurricane). The Europeans adopted the word that means 'god of the storm' because until they arrived in the Caribbean, they had never seen a storm like a hurricane."

Since my *abuela* loves to talk, that day she continued with the history lesson. She mentioned more Taíno words like *canoa* (canoe), *barbacoa* (barbecue), *maíz* (corn) y *patata* (potato). A lot of times I don't want to hear about all that my *abuela* wants to teach me, but in that lonely moment waiting out the storm, with only the wind and the rain to accompany my thoughts, I miss my *abuela* and her stories.

I wonder when my *papi* is going to return with news about her...

Chapter 16
Stefany

I watch TV all day and am constantly checking my phone for news about what's happening in Puerto Rico, and what I presume is happening with my family. I send a lot of texts and call many times, but no one answers. I'm worried not having heard from them.

Later on, in the afternoon, the doctor comes to the waiting room. I am sitting with my eyes closed and he startles me when he speaks:

"Ms. Ruiz, your sister is resting. Everything went well and the operation was a success. She's going to have to spend a few days more here to recuperate, but she'll be fine. A nurse will explain everything to you tomorrow. You can go see her in about a half an hour."

"Thank you for telling me, Dr. Álvarez. And thank you for taking good care of my sister."

Once again I sit in the uncomfortable chair, thankful for the information about my sister, but still worried.

Chapter 17
Kamila

Maggie Martin, grade 5

My *papi* returns after a couple of hours. The wind and the rain continue attacking everything, as they have for the last twelve hours or so. My *papi* comes into the house completely drenched. He looks awful, and not only for having been in the storm. Something happened. I know it.

Without saying anything, he grabs me and hugs me tight. And my *papi* starts to cry. He sobs. I have never heard anything like it from him in my whole life. I don't know what to say, so I ask him, "*Papi*, tell me. What happened?"

He lets go of me and with tears in his eyes he says to me, "Kami, your *abuela* died."

I try to catch my breath. I don't say anything.

It's not possible. My *abuela* is stubborn, yes, but she's strong. She can't be dead.

I think about the beautiful woman she is with her gray hair, talking to her birds. My *abuela*. My friend. I begin to cry and in that moment, only two questions come to mind: How? and Why?

*****

Later when I've calmed down a little, my *papi* explains what happened, or at least what he thinks happened. He found my *abuela* on the floor in the kitchen with a photo of her and her dear husband in her hand. It seems like she had a heart attack.

The wind is still blowing, though a little less than it was that morning. My *papi* offers me something to eat, but I decline. Though I'm only nine years old, this has been the worst day of my life. My *papi* then says to me:

"Kami, your *abuela* is with your *abuelo*. God is taking care of her now."

My *abuela* had so much faith in her religion and because of that, I know she will be okay. But, how is it going to be okay for me? For my *mami*? For my *tía*?

Chapter 18
Stefany

The day after the surgery, Susana looks better than she did before. That morning I find her in the same position as yesterday, but with so much more energy and much more color in her face.

"Stefany, how are you? Have you heard from Guillermo, Yolanda and *mamá*?"

"Hi, Susana. Good to see you with so much energy. How do you feel? No. I haven't heard anything. I'm going to call some friends who have other contacts in San Lorenzo. Maybe they will have some information," I say to her.

"Good idea. You poor thing. You must be so worried and here you are taking care of me," my sister says to me.

"Don't worry, Susana. Rest. I'm going to try to call again."

So, I leave my sister in the hospital bed and I take out my phone again to call my husband.

Chapter 19
Kamila

My *papi* and I sleep a little bit. For days, the rain continues along with the floods. It's not a good idea to leave the house, but my *papi* goes out to help the neighbors anyway. I see some men at a house trying to guide the water so it doesn't get in the house. But the situation seems futile with the amount of water that continues to fall from the sky.

Though it's still raining, from the window in the living room I can see my neighborhood where I used to walk and play. It's not anything like it was before.

That afternoon, after eating a little bit of beans that we heated up on the stove, I ask my *papi:*

"*Papi*, are the officials coming to help us?"

"What officials, Kamila?"

"The government officials. They always come when there's a disaster, right?"

"Normally, yes. But nobody knows what's going on. They say that the highways are destroyed and the trucks can't get through."

"But, how are we going to clean up the neighborhood and the town? There's a lot of trash because of all of the destruction."

"That's true. We are going to have to work together. It's going to be difficult for a little while."

"I'm not going to school?"

"No, *hija*. They say that the school has three feet of water. You won't have school for a while."

"*Papi*, can we go to *abuela*'s house to see the birds since *abuela* can't feed them?"

"When the rain stops for a bit, we'll go to her house. But now we have to work at our house. Can you help me?"

"Yes, *papi*."

I would like to spend more time thinking about my *abuela*, my friends and when I'm going to be able to listen to my music again, but I can't. My *papi* needs me. Instead of thinking about using my iPod I start to sing the Residente song and the other songs about Puerto Rico.

My whole world changed with the arrival of Hurricane Maria. She arrived, and with her she took another: my dear *abuela*, María Josefina Santos Bermúdez.

Chapter 20
Stefany

I finally receive a call from Guillermo five days after the storm, on September 25th. I am so happy to hear from him that I start to cry. I cry even harder when he tells me the other news.

"Stefany. Hi, *amor*[21]. How...?"

"Oh, Guillermo! You're okay. I'm so happy that you're okay. I've been so worried that I couldn't get in touch with you. How is Kamila? My *mamá*?"

"Stefany. I need to tell you something."

"Guillermo. Tell me. What happened?

"Your *mamá*..."

"What happened to my *mamá*? Did she fall? Is she in the hospital?"

"No, Stefany. Your *mamá* died during the storm. It seems like she had a heart attack."

I don't hear much else of what my husband says because the phone connection isn't that good, but still, I can't believe it. My *mamá*. The woman who had survived so many storms and assaults to the island, was dead. I am happy that my husband and daughter are safe, but the sadness that I feel for my *mamá* overcomes me. I cry hard, but I stop because I have to go tell my sister.

---

[21] amor: love, as a term of endearment.

I decide then to call my ex-brother-in-law to ask him for help. I have to return to Puerto Rico to be with my family.

What other challenges will I have to face?

Chapter 21
Kamila

Max Madron, grade 8

A week after the hurricane and still no signs from anyone from the government. The sun is once again shining and the air is clear. The storm has gone and now the amount of poverty that really exists in Puerto Rico is apparent. Not a single tree has leaves and the palm trees don't have any branches. What is left in the streets are huge holes and so much debris that the storm brought. When I'm outside with the neighbors, I hear the word "apocalypse" a lot. It's not a familiar word, but it has to mean what we are seeing now, an island stripped of its natural beauty.

My *mami* is still in Connecticut, because there are still no flights into San Juan. But, with Mr. Gómez's generator, a man from our neighborhood, I can charge my iPod and send her texts. I don't send her any photos because my *papi* says that I shouldn't waste the energy, but she probably doesn't want to see the destruction either.

Now in the mornings I get up and I go with my *papi* downtown. There we help other people who are doing what they can to serve the community.

"Good morning, *doña* Marta. How are you today?" I ask her when I give her a kiss on the cheek.
"Hi, Kamila. Thank you for coming again. What did you bring today?"
"More canned food and other things from the house."
"That's great, *hija*. Thank you. Come, help me prepare the food."

Doña Marta is a friend of my *abuela*. Like my *abuela*, she is really strong. After the storm she came to this building and started to organize the community. The first thing she did was to cook an enormous meal for everyone. Then people started to come and organize themselves.

At this new community center, when we are not

listening to the news on the WAPA radio station, there are musicians who come and play *bomba and plena*[22] to distract us. We spend a lot of time together, crying, laughing, complaining and dancing.

The adults talk a lot about politics and the governments, Puerto Rico's and the federal government, both of which seem to be forgetting about the Puerto Rican people. The adults keep saying things like, 'We are citizens' and ask, 'Where's the help?'

I spend every day with *doña* Marta and I play with the kids while their parents work. The children are happy. Me, too. Yes, I'm sad about my grandmother and the island, but I'm happy to be with people in my community. Like my grandmother and *doña* Marta and everyone else, I am strong. Puerto Rico will rise and I am going to help.

In the afternoon my *papi* finds me and asks me, "Kami, are you ready to go home?"
"Later, *papi*. I'm going to help *doña* Marta serve this food first."

I give my *papi* a hug and I get back to work.

I'm a worker. I'm *boricua*.

---

[22] bomba and plena: a style of music from Puerto Rico that features a lot of percussion

ABOUT THE AUTHOR

Jennifer Degenhardt taught high school Spanish for over 20 years and now teaches at the college level. At the time she realized her own high school students, many of whom had learning challenges, acquired language best through stories, so she began to write ones that she thought would appeal to them. She has been writing ever since.

Other titles by Jen Degenhardt available on Amazon:

La chica nueva | La Nouvelle Fille | <u>The New Girl</u>
La chica nueva (the ancillary/workbook
volume, Kindle book, audiobook)
Chuchotenango
El jersey | <u>The Jersey</u> | *Le Maillot*
La mochila | <u>The Backpack</u> | *Le sac à dos*
Moviendo montañas
La vida es complicada
Quince | <u>Fifteen</u>
El viaje difícil | *Un Voyage Difficile* | <u>A Difficult Journey</u>
La niñera
Fue un viaje difícil
Con (un poco de) ayuda de mis amigos
La última prueba
Los tres amigos | <u>Three Friends</u> | *Drei Freunde* | *Les Trois Amis*
María María: un cuento de un huracán | <u>María María: A Story of a Storm</u> | Maria Maria: un histoire d'un orage
Debido a la tormenta
La lucha de la vida | <u>The Fight of His Life</u>
Secretos
Como vuela la pelota

@JenniferDegenh1

@jendegenhardt9

@puenteslanguage &
World LanguageTeaching Stories (group)

Visit www.puenteslanguage.com to sign up to receive
information on new releases and other events.

Check out all titles as ebooks with audio on
www.digilangua.co.

CPSIA information can be obtained
at www.ICGtesting.com
Printed in the USA
LVHW050033090621
689708LV00012B/1503

9 780999 347966